MW01170854

The Free Inhabitants of the Several States; the Forgotten Proof WHO AFRICAN Americans Really Are.

By

Minister, Juan Monroe Wright El

1

Throughout my life, the biggest and most annoying issue that comes about ab initio, whether consciously by spewd racism or subconsciously by flaunting an atrocious attitude, is the question; Is the "Black" Man in America an American citizen? To answer this without hast, Yes he is. In fact, <u>the FULL opinion of the Dred Scott case</u> goes in depth on how and why. Thanks to one of the dissenting judges; Justice Curtis, who stated in his opinion which is binding on all lower courts: "So that, under the allegations contained in this plea, and admitted by the demurrer, the question is, whether any person of African descent, whose ancestors were sold as slaves in the United States, can be a citizen of the United States. **If any such person can be a citizen, this plaintiff has the right to the judgment of the court that he is so**; for no cause is shown by the plea why he is not so, except his descent and the slavery of his ancestors.

The first section of the second article of the Constitution 572*572 uses the language, "a citizen of the United States **at the time of** the adoption of the Constitution." One mode of approaching this question is, to inquire who were citizens of the United States at the time of the adoption of the Constitution.

Citizens of the United States at the time of the adoption of the Constitution can have been no other than citizens of the United States under the Confederation. By the Articles of Confederation, a Government was organized, the style whereof of was, **"The United States of America." This Government was in existence when the Constitution was framed and proposed for adoption,** and was to be superseded by the new Government of the United States of America, organized under the Constitution. When, therefore, the Constitution speaks of citizenship of the United States, existing at the time of the adoption of the Constitution, **it must necessarily refer to citizenship under the Government which existed prior to and at the time of such adoption.**

Without going into any question concerning the powers of the Confederation to govern the territory of the United States out of **the limits** of the States, and consequently to sustain the relation of Government and citizen in respect to **the inhabitants territory**, it may safely be said that **the citizens of the several States were citizens of the United States under the Confederation.**

That Government was simply **a confederacy of the several States**, possessing a few defined powers over subjects of general concern, each State retaining every power, jurisdiction, and right, not expressly delegated to the United States in

2

Congress assembled. And no power was thus delegated to the Government of the Confederation, to act on any question of citizenship, or to make any rules in respect thereto. The whole matter was left to stand upon the action of the several States, and to the natural consequence of such action, that the citizens of each State should be citizens of that Confederacy into which that State had entered, the style whereof was, **"The United States of America."**

To determine whether any **free persons, descended from Africans held in slavery**, were citizens of the United States under the Confederation, and consequently at the time of the adoption of the Constitution of the United States, it is only necessary to know whether any such persons were citizens of either of the States under the Confederation, at the time of the adoption of the Constitution.

Of this there can be no doubt. At the time of the ratification of the Articles of Confederation, **all free native-born inhabitants of the States of New Hampshire, Massachusetts, New 573*573 York, New Jersey, and North Carolina, though descended from African slaves**, were not only citizens of those States, but such of them as had the other necessary qualifications possessed the franchise of electors, on equal terms with other citizens....."

So far as stated , there's no disagreement with my answer. Justice Curtis continues: " The Supreme Court of North Carolina, in the case of the **State v. Manuel, (4 Dev. and Bat., 20,)** has declared the law of that State on this subject, in terms which I believe to be as sound law in the other States I have enumerated, as it was in North Carolina.

"According to the laws of this State," says Judge Gaston, in delivering the opinion of the court, "all human beings within it, who are not slaves, fall within one of two classes.

Whatever distinctions may have existed in the Roman laws between citizens and free inhabitants, **they are unknown to our institutions.** Before our Revolution, **all free persons born within the dominions of the King of Great Britain, whatever their color or complexion, were native-born British subjects** — those born out of his allegiance were aliens. **Slavery did not exist in England, but it did in the British colonies.** Slaves were not in legal parlance persons, but property. The moment the incapacity, the disqualification of slavery, was removed, **they became**

3

persons, and were then either British subjects, or not British subjects, according as they were or were not born within the allegiance of the British King. Upon the Revolution, **no other change** took place in the laws of **North Carolina** than was consequent on the transition from a colony dependent on a European King, to a free and sovereign State. Slaves remained slaves. **British subjects in North Carolina became North Carolina freemen. Foreigners, until made members of the State, remained aliens.** Slaves, manumitted here, **became freemen, and therefore, if born within North Carolina, are citizens of North Carolina, and all free persons born within the State are born citizens of the State.** The Constitution extended the elective franchise to **every freeman who had arrived at the age of twenty-one, and paid a public tax**; and it is a matter of universal notoriety, that, under it, free persons, without regard to color, **claimed and exercised the franchise**, until **it was taken from free men of color** a few years since by our amended Constitution." ....New York, by its Constitution of 1820, required colored persons to have some qualifications as prerequisites for voting, which white persons need not possess. And New Jersey, by its present Constitution, restricts the right to vote to white male citizens. But these changes can have no other effect upon the present inquiry, **except to show, that before they were made, no such restrictions existed; and colored in common with white persons, were not only citizens of those States, but entitled to the elective franchise on the same qualifications as white persons, as they now are in New Hampshire and Massachusetts.** I shall not enter into an examination of the existing opinions of that period respecting the African race, nor into any discussion concerning the meaning of those who asserted, in the Declaration of Independence, that **all men are created equal**; that they are endowed by their Creator with certain **inalienable rights**; that among these are life, liberty, and the pursuit of happiness. My own opinion is, that a calm comparison of these assertions of universal abstract truths, and of their own individual opinions and acts, would not leave 575*575 these men under any reproach of inconsistency; that the great truths they asserted on that solemn occasion, they were ready and anxious to make effectual,

4

wherever a necessary regard to circumstances, **which no statesman can disregard without producing more evil than good**, would allow; and that it would not be just to them, nor true in itself, to allege that they intended to say that the Creator of all men had endowed the white race, exclusively, with the great natural rights which the Declaration of Independence asserts. **But this is not the place to vindicate their memory.** As I conceive, we should deal here, not with such disputes if there can be a dispute concerning this subject, but with those **substantial facts** evinced by the written Constitutions of States, and by the notorious practice under them. And they show, in a manner which no argument can obscure, **that in some of the original thirteen States, free colored persons, before and at the time of the formation of the Constitution, were citizens of those States.**

The fourth of the fundamental articles of the Confederation was as follows: **"The free inhabitants of each of these States,** paupers, vagabonds, and fugitives from justice, excepted, **shall be entitled to all the privileges and immunities of free citizens in the several States."**

The **fact** that free persons of color were citizens of some of the several States, and the consequence, that this fourth article of the Confederation would have the effect to confer on such persons the privileges and immunities of general citizenship, were not only known to those who framed and adopted those articles, but the evidence is decisive, **that the fourth article was intended** to have that effect, and that more restricted language, which would have excluded such persons, was **deliberately and purposely rejected.**

On the 25th of June, 1778, the Articles of Confederation being under consideration by the Congress, the **delegates from South Carolina** moved to amend this fourth article, by inserting after the word **"free,"** and before the word **"inhabitants," the word "white,"** so that the privileges and immunities of general citizenship would be secured only to white persons. Two States voted for the amendment, eight States against it, and the vote of one State was divided. The language of the article **stood unchanged**, and both by its terms of inclusion, "free inhabitants," and the strong implication from its terms of exclusion, "paupers, vagabonds, and fugitives from justice," who alone were excepted, **it is clear, that**

5

under the Confederation, and at the time of the adoption of the Constitution, free colored persons of African descent might be, and, by reason of their citizenship in certain States, were entitled to the 576*576 privileges and immunities of general citizenship of the United States.

Did the Constitution of the United States deprive them or their descendants of citizenship?

That Constitution was ordained and established by the people of the United States, through the action, in each State, of those persons who were qualified by its laws to act thereon, in behalf of themselves and all other citizens of that State. In some of the States, as we have seen, **colored persons were among those qualified by law to act on this subject. These colored persons were not only included in the body of "the people of the United States," by whom the Constitution was ordained and established, but in at least five of the States they had the power to act, and doubtless did act, by their suffrages, upon the question of its adoption.** It would be strange, if we were to find in that instrument anything which deprived of their citizenship any part of the people of the United States who were among those by whom it was established.

I can find nothing in the Constitution which, proprio vigore, **deprives of their citizenship** any class of persons who were citizens of the United States at the time of its adoption, or who should be native-born citizens of any State after its adoption; **nor any power enabling Congress to disfranchise persons born on the soil of any State**, and entitled to citizenship of such State by its Constitution and laws. And my opinion is, that, under the Constitution of the United States, **every free person born on the soil of a State**, who is a citizen of that State by force of its Constitution or laws, **is** also a citizen of the United States.......**I will proceed to state the grounds of that opinion.**

The **first section of the second article of the Constitution** uses the language, "a **natural-born citizen.**" It thus assumes that citizenship may be acquired **by birth.** Undoubtedly, this language of the Constitution **was used in reference to** that principle of public law, well understood in this country at the time of the adoption of the Constitution, which referred citizenship to the place of birth. At the Declaration of Independence, and ever since, the received general doctrine has been, in conformity with the common law, **that free persons born within either of the colonies were subjects of the King**; that by the Declaration of

6

Independence, and the consequent acquisition of sovereignty by the several States, **all such persons ceased to be subjects, and became citizens of the several States**, except so far as some of them were **disfranchised by the legislative power of the States, or availed themselves**, seasonably, **of the right to adhere to the British Crown in the civil contest,** 577*577 and thus to **continue British subjects**. (McIlvain v. Coxe's Lessee, 4 Cranch, 209; Inglis v. Sailors' Snug Harbor, 3 Peters, p. 99; Shanks v. Dupont, Ibid, p. 242.)"

These are very eye opening facts presented here, to some, for the first time. Is it now clear the intent of King George's Royal Proclamation of 1763? The Justice continues; "It is a **substantive power**, distinct in its nature from all others; capable of affecting not only the relations of the States to the General Government, but of controlling the political condition of the people of the United States. **Certainly we ought to find this power granted by the Constitution**, at least by some necessary inference, **before we can say it does not remain to** the States or **the people**. I proceed therefore to examine all the provisions of the Constitution which may have some bearing on this subject. Among **the powers expressly granted to Congress is "the power to establish a uniform rule of naturalization."** It is not doubted that this is a power to prescribe a rule for the removal of the disabilities consequent on **foreign birth**. To hold that it extends further than this, **would do violence to the meaning of the term naturalization, fixed in the common law, (Co. Lit., 8 a, 129 a; 2 Ves., sen., 286; 2 Bl. Com., 293,)** and in the minds of those who concurred in framing and adopting the Constitution. It was in this sense of conferring on an alien and his issue the rights and powers of a native-born citizen, that it was employed in the Declaration of Independence. **It was in this sense it was expounded in the Federalist, (No. 42,) has been understood by Congress, by the Judiciary, (2 Wheat., 259, 269; 3 Wash. R., 313, 322; 12 Wheat., 277,) and by commentators on the Constitution. (3 Story's Com. on Con., 1 — 3; 1 Rawle on Con., 84 — 88; 1 Tucker's Bl. Com. App., 255 — 259.)**

It appears, then, that **the only power expressly granted to Congress** to legislate concerning citizenship, **is confined to** the removal of the disabilities of foreign birth.

Whether there be anything in the Constitution from which a broader power may be implied, will best be seen when we come to examine the two other

7

alternatives, which are, whether all free persons, born on the soil of the several States, **or** only such of them as may be citizens of each State, respectively, are thereby citizens of the United States. **The last of these alternatives, in my judgment, contains the truth.**

Undoubtedly, as has already been said, **it is a principle of public law**, recognised by the Constitution itself, **that birth on the soil of a country both creates the duties and confers the rights of citizenship**. But it must be remembered, that though 579*579 the Constitution was to form a Government, and under it **the United States of America were to be one united sovereign nation**, to which loyalty and obedience on the one side, and from which protection and privileges on the other, would be due, yet the several sovereign States, **whose people were then citizens,** were not only to continue in existence, **but with powers unimpaired**, except so far as they were granted by the people to the National Government.

Among the powers unquestionably possessed by the several States, was that of determining what persons should and what persons should not be citizens. It was practicable to confer on **the Government of the Union** this entire power. It embraced what may, well enough for the purpose now in view, be **divided into three parts**. First: The power to remove the disabilities of alienage, either by special acts in reference to each individual case, or by establishing a rule of naturalization to be administered and applied by the courts. Second: Determining what persons should enjoy the privileges of citizenship, in respect to the internal affairs of the several States. Third: What native-born persons should be citizens of the United States.

The first-named power, that of **establishing a uniform rule of naturalization**, was granted; and here the grant, according to its terms, stopped. Construing a Constitution containing only limited and defined powers of government, the argument derived from this definite and restricted power to establish a rule of naturalization, must be admitted to be exceedingly strong. I do not say it is necessarily decisive. **It might be controlled by other parts of the Constitution**. But when this particular subject of citizenship was under consideration, and, in the clause specially intended to define the extent of power concerning it, **we find a particular part of this entire power** separated from the residue, and **conferred on the General Government**, there arises a strong presumption that this is all which is granted, and **that the residue is left** to the States and **to the people**. And this presumption is, in my opinion, **converted into a certainty, by an examination of all such other clauses of the Constitution as touch this subject.**

I will examine each which can have any possible bearing on this question.

The first clause of the second section of the third article of the Constitution is, "The judicial power shall extend to controversies between a State and citizens of another State; between citizens of different States; between citizens of the same State, claiming lands under grants of different States; and between States, or the citizens thereof, and foreign States, 580*580 citizens, or subjects." **I do not think this clause has any considerable bearing upon the particular inquiry now under consideration.** Its purpose was, to extend the judicial power to those controversies into which local feelings or interests might so enter as to disturb the course of justice, or give rise to suspicions that they had done so, and **thus possibly give occasion to jealousy or ill will between different States, or a particular State and a foreign nation.** At the same time, I would remark, in passing, **that it has never been held,** I do not know that it has ever been supposed, **that any citizen of a State could bring himself under this clause and the eleventh and twelfth sections of the judiciary act of 1789, passed in pursuance of it, who was not a citizen of the United States.** But I have referred to the clause, **only** because it is one of the places where citizenship is mentioned by the Constitution. **Whether it is entitled to any weight in this inquiry or not, it refers only to citizenship of the several States; it recognises that; but it does not recognise citizenship of the United States as something distinct therefrom.**

As has been said, the purpose of this clause did not necessarily connect it with citizenship of the United States, even if that were something distinct from citizenship of the several States, in the contemplation of the Constitution. This cannot be said of other clauses of the Constitution, which I now proceed to refer to.

"The citizens of each State shall be entitled to all the privileges and immunities of citizens of the several States." **Nowhere else in the Constitution is there anything concerning a general citizenship; but here,** privileges and immunities to be enjoyed throughout the United States, under and by force of the national compact, are granted and secured. In selecting those who are to enjoy these national rights of citizenship, how are they described? **As citizens of each State.** It is to them these national rights are secured. The qualification for them is not to be looked for in any provision of the Constitution or laws of the United States. They are to be citizens of the several States, and, as such, the privileges and immunities of general citizenship, derived from and guarantied by the Constitution, are to be enjoyed by them. It would seem that if it had been intended to constitute a class of native-born persons within the States, who should derive their citizenship of the United States from the action of the Federal Government, this was an occasion for referring to them. It cannot be supposed that it was the purpose of this article to confer the privileges and immunities of citizens in all the States upon persons not citizens of the United States.

581*581 And if it was intended to secure these rights only to citizens of the United States, how has the Constitution here described such persons? **Simply as citizens of each State.**

But, further: though, as I shall presently more fully state, I do not think the enjoyment of the elective franchise essential to citizenship, there can be no doubt **it is one of the chiefest attributes of citizenship under the American Constitutions; and the just and constitutional possession of this right is decisive evidence of citizenship.** The provisions made by a Constitution on this subject must therefore be looked to as bearing directly on the question what persons are citizens under that Constitution; and as being decisive, to this extent, that all such persons as are allowed by the Constitution to exercise the elective franchise, and thus to participate in the Government of the United States, must be deemed citizens of the United States.

Here, again, the consideration presses itself upon us, that if there was designed to be a particular class of native-born persons within the States, deriving their citizenship from the Constitution and laws of the United States, they should at least have been referred to as those by whom the President and House of Representatives were to be elected, and to whom they should be responsible.

Instead of that, we again find this subject referred to the laws of the several States. The electors of President are to be appointed in such manner as the Legislature of each State may direct, and the qualifications of electors of members of the House of Representatives shall be the same as for electors of the most numerous branch of the State Legislature.

Laying aside, then, the case of aliens, concerning which the Constitution of the United States has provided, and confining our view to free persons born within the several States, we find that the Constitution has recognised the general principle of public law, that allegiance and citizenship depend on the place of birth; that it has not attempted practically to apply this principle by designating the particular classes of persons who should or should not come under it; that when we turn to the Constitution for an answer to the question, what free persons, born within the several States, are citizens of the United States, the only answer we can receive from any of its express provisions is, the citizens of the several States are to enjoy the privileges and immunities of citizens in every State, and their franchise as electors under the Constitution depends on their citizenship in the several States. Add to this, that the Constitution was ordained by the citizens of the several States; that they were "the people of the United States," for whom 582*582 and whose posterity the Government was declared in the preamble of the Constitution to be made; that each of them was "a citizen of the United States at the time of the adoption of the Constitution," within the meaning of those words in that instrument; that by them the Government was to be and was in fact organized; and that no power is conferred on the Government of the Union to discriminate between them, or to disfranchise any of them — the necessary conclusion is, that those persons born within the several States, who, by force of their respective Constitutions and laws, are citizens of the State, are thereby citizens of the United States.

It may be proper here to notice some supposed objections to this view of the subject.

It has been often asserted that the Constitution was made exclusively by and for the white race. It has already been shown that in five of the thirteen original States, colored persons then possessed the elective franchise, and were among those by whom the Constitution was ordained and established. If so, it is not true, in point of fact, that the Constitution was made exclusively by the white race. And that it was made exclusively for the white race is, in my opinion, not only an assumption not warranted by anything in the Constitution, but contradicted by its opening declaration, that it was ordained and established by the people of the United States, for themselves and their posterity. And as free colored persons

11

were then citizens of at least five States, and so in every sense part of the people of the United States, they were among those for whom and whose posterity the Constitution was ordained and established.....

There is one view of this article entitled to consideration in this connection. It is manifestly copied from **the fourth of the Articles of Confederation**, with only slight changes of phraseology, which render its meaning more precise, **and dropping the clause which excluded paupers, vagabonds, and fugitives from justice**, probably because these cases could be dealt with under the police powers of the States, and a special provision therefor was not necessary. It has been suggested, that in adopting it into the Constitution, **the words "free inhabitants" were changed for the word "citizens."** An examination of the forms of expression commonly used in the State papers of that day, and an attention to the substance of this article of the Confederation, will show that the words "free inhabitants," as then used, **were synonymous with citizens.** When the Articles of Confederation were adopted, we were in the midst **of the war of the Revolution, and there were very few persons then embraced in the words "free inhabitants," who were not born on our soil. It was not a time when many, save the 585*585 children of the soil, were willing to embark their fortunes in our cause;** and though there might be an inaccuracy in the uses of words to call free inhabitants citizens, it was then a technical rather than a substantial difference. If we **look into the Constitutions and State papers of that period**, we find the inhabitants or people of these colonies, or the inhabitants of this State, or Commonwealth, employed to designate those whom we should now denominate citizens. The substance and purpose of the article **prove it was in this sense it used these words**: it secures to the free inhabitants of each State the privileges and immunities of free citizens in every State. It is not conceivable that the States should have agreed to extend the privileges of citizenship to persons not entitled to enjoy the privileges of citizens in the States where they dwelt; that under this article there was a class of persons in some of the States, not citizens, to whom were secured all the privileges and immunities of citizens when they went into other States; and the just conclusion

12

is, that though the Constitution cured an inaccuracy of language, **it left the substance of this article in the National Constitution the same as it was in the Articles of Confederation.**

The history of this fourth article, respecting the attempt to exclude free persons of color from its operation, has been already stated. It is reasonable to conclude **that this history was known to those who framed and adopted the Constitution.** That under this fourth article of the Confederation, **free persons of color might be entitled to the privileges of general citizenship,** if otherwise entitled thereto, **is clear.** When this article was, in substance, placed in and made part of the Constitution of the United States, with no change in its language calculated to exclude free colored persons from the benefit of its provisions, the presumption is, to say the least, strong, **that the practical effect which it was designed to have, and did have, under the former Government, it was designed to have, and should have, under the new Government.**

It may be further objected, **that if free colored persons may be citizens of the United States, it depends only on the will of a master whether he will emancipate his slave, and thereby make him a citizen. Not so.** The master is subject to the will of the State. Whether he shall be allowed to emancipate his slave at all; if so, on what conditions; and what is to be the political status of the freed man, depend, not on the will of the master, but on the will of the State, upon which the political status of all its native-born inhabitants depends. Under the Constitution of the United States, each State has retained this power of determining the political status of its native-born 586*586 inhabitants, and no exception thereto can be found in the Constitution. And if a master in a slaveholding State should carry his slave into a free State, and there emancipate him, he would not thereby make him a native-born citizen of that State, and consequently no privileges could be claimed by such emancipated slave as a citizen of the United States. For, **whatever powers the States may exercise to confer privileges of citizenship on persons not born on their soil, the Constitution of the United States-does not recognise such citizens.** As has already been said, it recognises the great principle of public law, that allegiance and citizenship spring from the place of birth. It leaves to the States the application of that principle to individual cases. It secured to the citizens of each State the privileges and immunities of citizens in every other State. **But it does not allow to the States the power to** make aliens citizens,

13

or permit one State to take persons born on the soil of another State, and, contrary to the laws and policy of the State where they were born, make them its citizens, and so citizens of the United States. No such deviation from the great rule of public law was contemplated by the Constitution; and when any such attempt shall be actually made, it is to be met by applying to it those rules of law and those principles of good faith which will be sufficient to decide it, **and not,** in my judgment, **by denying that all the free native-born inhabitants of a State,** who are its citizens under its Constitution and laws, **are also citizens of the United States.**

It has sometimes been urged that colored persons are shown not to be citizens of the United States by the fact that the naturalization laws apply **only to white persons.** But whether a person born in the United States be or be not a citizen, **cannot depend on laws which refer only to aliens,** and do not affect the status of persons born in the United States. The utmost effect which can be attributed to them is, to show that Congress has not deemed it expedient generally to apply the rule to colored aliens. That they might do so, if thought fit, is clear. The Constitution has not excluded them. And since that has conferred the power on Congress to naturalize colored aliens, **it certainly shows color is not a necessary qualification for citizenship under the Constitution of the United States.** It may be added, that **the power to make colored persons citizens of the United States, under the Constitution,** has been **actually exercised** in repeated and important instances. **(See the Treaties with the Choctaws, of September 27, 1830, art. 14; with the Cherokees, of May 23, 1836, art. 12; Treaty of Guadalupe Hidalgo, February 2, 1848, art. 8.)**....It would be strange, if laws were found on our statute book to that effect, when, by solemn treaties, **large bodies of Mexican and North American Indians as well as free colored inhabitants of Louisiana have been admitted to citizenship of the United States.**

The conclusions at which I have arrived on this part of the case are:

First. That the free native-born citizens of each State **are** citizens of the United States.

Second. That as **free colored persons** born within some of the States **are citizens of those States,** such persons **are also citizens of the United States.**

Third. That **every such citizen**, residing in any State, **has the right to sue and is**

14

liable to be sued in the Federal courts, as a citizen of that State in which he resides.

Fourth. That as the plea to the jurisdiction in this case shows **no facts,** except that the plaintiff was of African descent, and his ancestors were sold as slaves, and **as these facts are not inconsistent with his citizenship of the United States,** and his residence in the State of Missouri, the plea to the jurisdiction was bad, and the judgment of the Circuit Court overruling it was correct.

I dissent, therefore, **from that part of the opinion** of the majority of the court, **in which it is held that a person of African descent cannot be a citizen of the United States;** and I regret I must go further, **and dissent both from** what I deem **their assumption of authority to examine the constitutionality of the act of Congress commonly called the Missouri compromise 589*589 act, and the grounds and conclusions announced in their opinion.**

The residence of the plaintiff in the State of Illinois, and **the residence of himself and his wife in the territory acquired from France lying north of latitude thirty-six degrees thirty minutes, and north of the State of Missouri,** are each relied on by the plaintiff in error. As **the residence in the territory affects the plaintiff's wife and children as well as himself,** I must inquire what was its effect..."

Justice Curtis elaborated on this aspect of "Black" people having dominion **in the Territory** ; "By the **act of April 20, 1836, (4 Stat. at Large, 10,)** passed in the same month and year of the removal of the plaintiff to Fort Snelling, this part of **the territory ceded by France,** where Fort Snelling is, **together with so much of the territory of the United States east of the Mississippi as now constitutes the State of Wisconsin, was brought under a Territorial Government, under the name of the Territory of Wisconsin. By the eighteenth section of this act,** it was enacted, "That **the inhabitants of this Territory** shall be entitled to and enjoy all and singular the rights, privileges, and advantages, granted and secured **to the people of the Territory of the United States northwest of the river Ohio, by the articles of compact contained in the ordinance for the government of said Territory, passed on the 13th day of July, 1787; and shall be subject to all the restrictions and prohibitions in said articles of compact imposed upon the people of the said Territory."** The sixth article of that compact is, "there shall be neither slavery nor

15

involuntary servitude in the said Territory, otherwise than in 593*593 the punishment of crimes, whereof the party shall have been duly convicted. Provided, always, that any person escaping into the same, from whom labor or service is lawfully claimed in any one of the original States, such fugitive may be lawfully reclaimed, and conveyed to the person claiming his or her labor or service, as aforesaid." **By other provisions of this act establishing the Territory of Wisconsin, the laws of the United States, and the then existing laws of the State of Michigan, are extended over the Territory;** the latter being subject to alteration and repeal by the legislative power of the Territory created by the act..I proceed then to inquire **what the rules of international law prescribe concerning the change of status of the plaintiff wrought by the law of the Territory of Wisconsin.**

It is generally agreed by writers upon international law, and the rule has been judicially applied in a great number of cases, that wherever any question may arise concerning the status of a person, **it must be determined according to that law which has next previously rightfully operated on and fixed that status.** And, further, that the laws of a country do not rightfully operate upon and fix the status of **persons who are within its limits in itinere, or who are abiding there for definite temporary purposes, as for health, curiosity, or occasional business;** that these laws, known to writers on public and private international law as personal statutes, **operate only on the inhabitants of the country.** Not that it is or can be denied that each independent nation may, if it thinks fit, apply them to all persons within their limits. But when this is done, not in conformity with the principles of international law, other States are not understood to be willing to recognise or allow effect to such applications of personal statutes....But **it must have been apparent, both to the framers of the Constitution and the people of the several States** who were to act upon it, that the Government thus provided for could not continue, **unless** the Constitution should confer on the United States the necessary powers to continue it. That temporary Government, under the ordinance, was to consist of certain officers, to be appointed by and responsible to **the Congress of the Confederation; their powers had been conferred and defined by the ordinance.** So far as it provided for the temporary government of the

16

Territory, it was an ordinary act of legislation, deriving its force from the legislative power of Congress, and **depending for its vitality upon the continuance of that legislative power.** But the officers to be appointed for the Northwestern Territory, after the adoption of the Constitution, must necessarily be officers of the United States, and not of the Congress of the Confederation; appointed and commissioned by the President, and **exercising powers derived from the United States under the Constitution.**

Such was the relation between the United States and the Northwestern Territory, which all reflecting men must have foreseen would exist, when the Government created by the 607*607 Constitution should supersede that of the Confederation. That if the new Government should be without power to govern this Territory, it could not appoint and commission officers, and send them into the Territory, to exercise there legislative, judicial, and executive power; and that this Territory, which was even then foreseen to be so important, both politically and financially, to all the existing States, must be left not only without the control of the General Government, in respect to its future political relations to the rest of the States, but absolutely **without any Government, save what its inhabitants, acting in their primary capacity, might from time to time create for themselves....**It would seem, also, that when we find the subject-matter of the growth and formation and admission of new States, and the disposal of the territory for these ends, were under consideration, and that some provision therefor was expressly made, it is improbable that it would be, in its terms, a grossly inadequate provision; and that an indispensably necessary power to institute temporary Governments, and to legislate for the inhabitants of the territory, was passed silently by, and left to be deduced from the necessity of the case.

In the argument at the bar, great attention has been paid to the meaning of the word "territory."

Ordinarily, when the territory of a sovereign power is spoken of, it refers to that tract of country which is under the political jurisdiction of that sovereign power. Thus Chief Justice Marshall (in United States v. Bevans, 3 Wheat., 386) says: "What, then, is the extent of jurisdiction which a State possesses? We answer, without hesitation, **the jurisdiction of a State is coextensive with its territory."** Examples might easily be multiplied of this use of the word, but they are unnecessary, because it is familiar. But **the word "territory" is not used in this broad and general sense in this clause of the Constitution.**

At the time of the adoption of the Constitution, the United States held a great tract of country northwest of the Ohio; another tract, then of unknown extent, ceded by South Carolina; and a confident expectation was then entertained, and afterwards realized, that they then were or would become the owners of other great tracts, claimed by North Carolina and Georgia. These ceded tracts lay within the limits of the United States, and out of the limits of any particular State; and **the cessions embraced the civil and political jurisdiction,** and so much of the soil as had not previously been granted to individuals....It has already been stated, that after the Government of the United States was organized under the Constitution, the temporary Government of the Territory northwest of the river Ohio could no longer exist, **save under the powers conferred on Congress by the Constitution.** Whatever legislative, judicial, or executive authority should be exercised therein could be derived only from the people of the United States under the Constitution. **And, accordingly, an act was passed on the 617*617 7th day of August, 1789, (1 Stat. at Large, 50,) which recites:** "Whereas, in order that the ordinance of the United States in Congress assembled, for the government of **the territory northwest of the river Ohio, may continue to have full effect,** it is required that certain provisions should be made, so as to adapt the same to the present Constitution of the United States." It then provides for the appointment by the President of all officers, who, by force of the ordinance, were to have been appointed by the Congress of the Confederation, and their commission in the manner required by the Constitution; and empowers the Secretary of the Territory to exercise the powers of the Governor in case of the death or necessary absence of the latter...**Congress has erected Governments over Territories acquired from France and Spain.**....The second section of the sixth article is, "This Constitution, and the laws of the United States which shall be made in pursuance thereof, and **all treaties made** or which shall be made **under the authority of the United States, shall be the supreme law of the land."** This has made treaties part

18

of our municipal law;..." , Futher, Justice Catron adds: "**The King of Great Britain, by his proclamation of 1763**, virtually claimed that the country west of the mountains had been conquered from France, and ceded to the Crown of Great Britain by the treaty of Paris of that year, and he says: "**We reserve it under our sovereignty, protection, and dominion, for the use of the Indians.**" This country was **conquered from** the Crown of Great Britain, and **surrendered to the United States by the treaty of peace of 1783.** The colonial charters of **Virginia, North Carolina, and Georgia, included it.** Other States set up pretensions of claim to some portions of the territory north of the Ohio, but they were of no value, as I suppose. (5 Wheat., 375.) And how does the power of Congress stand west of the Mississippi river? The country there was acquired **from France, by treaty, in 1803.** It declares, that the First Consul, in the **name of the French Republic,** doth hereby **cede to the United States, in full sovereignty, the colony or province of Louisiana, with all the rights and appurtenances of the said territory.** And, by article third, that "the **inhabitants of the ceded territory shall be incorporated in the Union of the United States,** and admitted as soon as possible, according to the principles of the Federal Constitution, **to the enjoyment of all the rights, advantages, and immunities, of citizens of the United States; and, in the mean time, they shall be maintained and protected in the free enjoyment of their liberty, property, and the religion which they profess.**" For more on this, read; John Jay's Letter to the Oppressed Inhabitants of Canada/New France/Province of Quebec.

Justice McLean adds; ". On the question of citizenship, it must be admitted that we have not been very fastidious. **Under the late treaty with Mexico(Spain), we have made citizens of all grades, combinations, and colors. The same was done in the admission of Louisiana(France) and Florida(Spain). No one ever doubted, and no court ever held, that the people of these Territories did not become citizens under the treaty.** They have exercised all the rights of citizens, without being naturalized under the acts of Congress."

Those free "colored" inhabitants acquired from **Mexico, West and East**

Florida via Spain(New Spain 1521-1821), and from **Upper and Lower Louisiana**

via France(New France 1534-1763) are properly the **Mauri people of Ancient Mauretania**(Morocco) known during the European Colonial period as Moors, Moriscos, Seminoles, Negroes(1) and Indians(Barbary States). During this same time period, **Ancient Mauretania is called the Barbary Coast.** Though unfortunate, politically a mass of these people are called Negroes or African Americans in this modern time, **a great race of people they are.** Able to boast illustrious heritage as early as the date of **the archaeological find of the melanated Mummy named "Lucy"** to their **Punic ancestors**, the Fathers of sea commerce, or a slew of **Muslim dynasties** enlightening Europeans in the Dark Age and falling out of God's favor **West of the Mississippi in Muslim Spain**(Granada/Hebrew's Sepharad). Which brings me to this. With the help of the Justices' opinion from the Dred Scott case above cited, we see that **the free inhabitants were here in North America prior to the formation of the Union of the Constitution or the Confederation under the Articles of Confederation.** The United States of America acquired land then that is today embraced under its swollen umbrella of jurisdiction from **Spain, France and Britain.** One now should asked, who ceded them the land via treaty or otherwise? This leads to a series of more monographs I shall produce for our preservation of that part of history which we should never forget.

(1)"**Thus an act was passed in Massachusetts on the 6th of March, 1788, forbidding any Negro not a subject of the emperor of Morocco, or a citizen of the United States, from tarrying in the Commonwealth."** Click here to see

That makes all African Americans **properly** Moorish Americans, made in this USA as first class citizens. Knowing, the etymology of **Black describing a person** finds its origin in the **1540s** term Blackamoor. That is within the same time the Spanish and French colonies of **New Spain and New France were located on the North American landmass,**. Moor being the pronoun and also in the late 14th century meaning "**North African, Berber**", from the Latin Maurus meaning"**inhabitant of Mauretania**"(northwest Africa) and it also states,"Being a

dark people **in relation to Europeans**, their name in the Middle Ages was **a** synonym for Negro...".<u>Source is Here Click here.</u>

Now we must show Morocco in the position of ceding land to Spain, France and Britain **either by treaty or otherwise.** My research is extended into years on this subject and here is my conclusion in the form of **points in reference to each nation,** giving not too much attention to one over the other;

1. As to Spain and its Moorish roots, thanks to **Tariq ibn Ziyad in 711** with his reconquest of Spain (**the inhabitants of Spain at that time were mainly Mauri via Carthage; Hispania is a byproduct of the Punic Wars 264 -146 BC**) . Spain's attachment of Moorish dominions is the result of the Fall of Granada in 1492. Then, move to 1493, when **Pope Alexander VI "divides" the New World(America) between Spain(North America) and Portugal(South America).** *Source:"Chronology of U.S. History, pg.56 of The Universal Almanac 1996, Andrew and McMeel".* That puts Spain in possession of North America. New Spain established 1521.

2. As to France, according to **pg.50 of A Savage Empire: Trappers, Traders, Tribes, and the Wars That Made America by Alan Axelrod(2011),** "Verrazzano's voyage convinced the king to seek to establish a colony in the newly discovered land. Verazzano gave the names **Francesca** and **Nova Gallia** to that land **between New Spain(Mexico) and English Newfoundland.**" And in **1534 Jacques Cartier** planted a cross in the Gaspe Peninsula and claimed the land in the name of King Francis I, Source: **pg.36 of A Brief History of Canada by Roger E. Riendeau (2007).**

3. As for England or shall I say Britain, their ties to this land Morocco comes via **the Barbary Company also called Marocco Company. A trade company established by England's Queen Elizabeth I in1585** through a patent granted to 40 people including **the Earls of Warwick and Leicester.** And a treaty signed at Mequinez in1728 stated, "**that Moors, Jews, and other**

natives of Marocco in the service of British subjects there should be exempt from taxes of all kinds." Source: **pg 236 of The Early Chartered Companies (A.D.1296-1858) Parts 1296-1858, by George Cawston, Augustus Henry Keane.**

Therefor, today's African American is none other than a Moor proper. Thus, **he is a citizen of the soil of the northwest antebellum Africa.** It is my strong opinion, being domiciled in the territory Northwest of the Ohio, that the several States in reference to the free inhabitant Moors may be referring to the "Barbary" States properly Morocco of the farthest West, that's al-Mahgreb al-aqsa in Arabic. I might suggest the reader in looking further into the Spanish and French Protectorate of Morocco, Sephardic Jews and also article XV of the convention of Madrid of 1880, Noble Drew Ali, the Barbary Treaty collection, the Moriscos, HR 75 of 1933, the Seminoles, Canaanites, the Gullah, the Wisconsin Glacial Period, Mississippian Culture, Olmec, Aztecs, the Beaver Wars, the Five Civilized Tribes, the Maroons, Granny(Queen) Nanny, John Horse, the Inca Jews, the events known as the "Scramble for Africa",the Continental Association(1774), the Sambo Naga People of Borobudur, the Declaration on Rights of Indigenous Peoples, evidence of ancient Egyptians in America and my favorites, The International Decade for the People of African Descent 2015-2024(UN), the Teutonic plates and the Flora (especially rice) and Fauna shared between the east coast of America(South Carolina) and the west coast of Africa(Sierra Leone). All subjects mentioned above is your heritage.

Thank yourselves for reading this later as it will benefit you and your Family.

 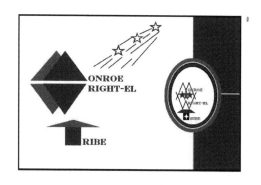

23

I, being hand in hand with the Most High in constructing this work., am blessed to having been chosen to undertake this magnanimous mission. Thank You.

From, Minister of Indigenous Awareness Ministry of the Breath,

Grand Chief of the Monroe Wright El Tribe,

Juan Monroe Wright El, Sui Juris

I close with this one extra thing. The Supreme Court in 1922, interpreted the federal laws restricting citizenship as allowing only whites and blacks of African descent to become citizens; see Ozawa v United States,260 U.S.178(1922).

And finally from page 74 of the book, "13th Tribe" by Arthur Koestler, where he tracks the linguistic travels of the biblical Jews. He states, "Incidentally, the descendants of the biblical Tribes are the classic example of linguistic adaptability. First they spoke Hebrew; in the Babylonian exile, Chaldean; at the time of Jesus(Yeshua), Aramaic; in Alexandria, Greek; in Spain, Arabic but later Ladino- a Spanish-Hebrew mixture, written in Hebrew characters, the Sephard equivalent to Yiddish; and so it goes on. They preserved their religious identity, but changed languages at their convenience. The Khazars were not descended from the Tribes, but, as we have seen, they shared a certain cosmopolitanism and other social characteristics with their co-religionists. "

24

Hyperlinks Used

On Page 3; www.law.cornell.edu/supremecourt/text/60/393#writing-USSC_CR_0060_0393_ZD1

On Page 20; http:avalon.law.yale.edu/18th_century/contcong_05-29-75.asp#2

On Page 21-22; www.archive.org/details/actsresolvespass178889mass ,

www.etymonline.com/index.php?allowed_in_frame=0&search=Blackamoor ,

www.etymonline.com/index.php?allowed_in_frame=0&search=Moor

On Page 23; www.avalon.law.edu/subject_menus/barmenu.asp

On Page 23; www.un.org/en/events/africandescentdecade/ ,

www.wondermondo.com/SierraLeone.htm .

All Government documents and other sources used in this monograph are available for free.

This literary work was authored by Minister Juan Monroe Wright-El, sui juris, TTEE, for Indigenous Awareness Ministry of the Breath a 508 Ministry Trust.

Made in the USA
Columbia, SC
11 March 2024

32461781R00017